Tanka Society of America

Founded in 2000

Official Website: www.tankasocietyofamerica.org

Ribbons **Editor:** Susan Weaver
127 N. 10th St., Allentown, PA 18102; ribbonseditor@gmail.com

Tanka Cafe Editor: Michael McClintock
1830 N. Bush Ave., Clovis, CA 93619; MchlMcClintock@aol.com

Tanka Prose Editor: Liz Lanigan
38 McClure St., EVATT ACT 2617, Australia
tankaproseeditor@gmail.com

President and Webperson: Michael Dylan Welch
22230 N.E. 28th Pl., Sammamish, WA 98074-6408; welchm@aol.com

Vice President: Susan Burch
9128 Cool Hollow Terr., Hagerstown, MD 21740; sehbtree@yahoo.com

Secretary: Kathabela Wilson
439 S. Catalina Ave. #306, Pasadena, CA 91106; poetsonsite@gmail.com

Treasurer: James Won
6233 Golden West, Temple City, CA 91780; jameswon@charter.net

Cover: *Jewel Bug*, Oil pastels on paper, 16 x 12, by Hemapriya Chellapan

Cover Design: Kathleen Sue Mallari

D1476852

Submission Guidelines: See last pages of journal.

Business Address: 439 S. Catalina Ave. #306, Pasadena, CA 91106

Ribbons: **Tanka Society of America Journal**, published triannually in Winter, Spring/Summer, and Fall. All prior copyrights are retained by contributors, and full rights revert back on publication. Neither the TSA, its officers, nor the *Ribbons* editor assume responsibility for views of any contributors (including TSA officers) whose work is printed in *Ribbons*.

TSA Memberships include three issues of the Tanka Society of America's journal, *Ribbons*. One-year membership in USD: $30 USA; $35 Canada and Mexico; $42 elsewhere. Make all checks or money orders payable to the Tanka Society of America and mail to Kathabela Wilson, TSA Secretary, 439 S. Catalina Ave. #306, Pasadena, CA 91106.

Additional copies of recent issues of *Ribbons* may be ordered from our production partner at www.amazon.com. (Payment by PayPal is available from Amazon.) For questions about payment for non-US residents, contact Kathabela Wilson by email: poetsonsite@gmail.com.

ISSN: 2150-4954

RIBBONS

Spring/Summer 2021: Volume 17, Number 2

CONTENTS

The Back Cover

The human condition depends largely on the environment, and tanka generally juxtapose these two concepts—the human condition and the environment—to show how one relates to the other, both evoking emotion and enhancing understanding. Because not only does the environment affect the human condition, the human condition also affects the environment.

For the back cover, I've chosen a tanka by Marcyn Del Clements that aptly and humorously describes the human condition as affected by our environment.

> every time I think
> I have a handle on things . . .
> a door's left unlocked
> a window's left ajar
> my skirt's up in back

Marcyn Del Clements, Claremont, CA

The fifth line, *my skirt's up in back,* which seems to me to be the female equivalent of the unzipped zipper for the male of the species, sold me immediately on this tanka. And, of course, who among us has not often wondered, as soon as we've left the house, whether we have forgotten to turn off the burner on the stove, locked the front door, or closed the storm windows?

I asked Marcy (as she signs herself) what prompted her to write this tanka, what was going on in her head, how she was feeling when she wrote it, how much of it was real, and to tell me a little about herself. Here is what she said . . .

"Gosh! It just came because it was all real. I guess I was feeling frustrated, compiling all the things I forget to do. I try to lock the house and set the alarm when I leave. A couple times, I've come back and the front door is unlocked and unbolted! 'Course the alarm would go off right away if anyone came in. But it's just *huh!!!* and if you set the alarm and one slider is a crack open, the alarm is armed, but a good earthquake, like we have sometimes, would set it off.

"My husband died ten years ago, and I'm still trying to keep it together. Because I want to live in my house, my beautiful home, till they have to carry me out feet first! So I try to keep it together. Feed my fish, wash the dishes, get enough sleep. Speaking of which, I need to hit the hay."

The style of this tanka is a simple setup in lines one and two, followed by a series of three payoffs, the last one, line five, being the killer line. It's purely a story of human foibles. The best of intentions gone awry. *There oughta be a law!*

– *Michael H. Lester*

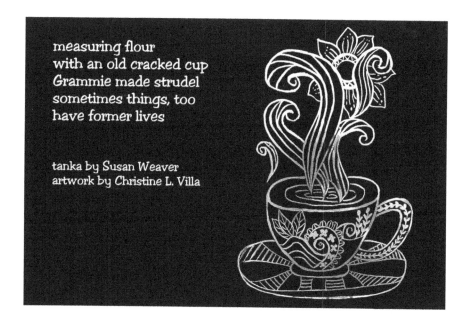

measuring flour
with an old cracked cup
Grammie made strudel
sometimes things, too
have former lives

tanka by Susan Weaver
artwork by Christine L. Villa

President's Message

Well, it's late spring in the United States, and many people are receiving their vaccinations. It may still be a long time before we can all feel like we're back to normal, but in the meantime perhaps this sabbatical of sorts has been a reminder of what we too easily take for granted. The plus side, for many, has been Zoom meetings that let us attend events across the country or across the world, where we can meet new people and make new poetry friends. In our tanka we've recorded all our pandemic changes, all these ups and downs. And we'll continue to do so, even while many of us might wish for other subjects to dominate our consciousness and perhaps our poems.

I look forward, as always, to seeing where we'll take tanka next. Speaking of spring, I read this poem by Yosano Akiko, in *The Penguin Book of Japanese Verse* by Geoffrey Bownas and Anthony Thwaite:

> Spring is short:
> Why ever should it
> Be thought immortal?
> I grope for
> My full breasts with my hands.

With a different sort of spring in mind, perhaps this poem by Itō Sachio (also from the Penguin book) speaks to the wonderful variety of tanka possible from our members, even if we're not cowherds:

> When cowherds begin
> To make poems,
> Many new styles
> In the world
> Will spring up.

I'm pleased to welcome Susan Weaver as our new *Ribbons* editor, embracing both new and old styles of tanka. As part of the transition from Christine L. Villa as our previous editor, Susan has benefited from the help of Michael H. Lester, who edited this issue's selected tanka and sequences. We're also fortunate to have Liz Lanigan as our new tanka prose editor. I know you'll enjoy all their selections and other highlights throughout this issue.

A nod of thanks, too, to Ryland Li. He has initiated a new Young Adults Tanka Group, for poets under age forty. If you're interested, please contact him at li.ryland@gmail.com (open to anyone, whether you're a TSA member or not).

By the time you read this, Autumn Noelle Hall and Don Miller will be busy reviewing submissions for the 2021 Sanford Goldstein International Tanka Contest, and we look forward to their selections. From June 15 to July 31, be sure to submit to our 2021 TSA members' anthology, to be edited by Michael H. Lester.

A little heads-up is that by this fall the TSA website hosting service through Google Sites is migrating to a new system, meaning that our existing website will have a makeover. We'll keep you posted with developments, but expect it to have a different look, even while all the content should stay the same. Two advantages of this change will be increased security and greater compatibility with mobile devices and tablets. Meanwhile, watch for more TSA news via email and on social media, and thank you for your continuing passion for tanka poetry.

– Michael Dylan Welch

Editor's Message

Welcome to the Spring/Summer issue of *Ribbons*, and thank you to all who contributed poetry, art, essays, reviews and, along with them, something of yourselves.

With this issue, I am honored to take the helm of this journal that I both respect and enjoy reading. Since I joined The Tanka Society of America in 2015, searching for a new writing voice in retirement, *Ribbons* has welcomed me to a community of poets and taught me much about tanka. In fact, I found more opportunities to learn than I thought possible. This new role is yet one more. I thank our previous editor, Christine Villa, for saying more than once, "You could do this," for giving me the chance, and helping me along the way. And for the support and example of her long-time predecessor, David Rice. Both have left big shoes to fill.

I also want to recognize the editorial team, who've put in extra effort to ease the transition.

To give me time to plan ahead, Chrissi arranged for Michael H. Lester to select and edit tanka and tanka sequences for this issue. A fine tanka poet with awards in three consecutive Sanford Goldstein contests, he has been great to work with and generous with his time, despite the demands of his active Los Angeles practice as a CPA and attorney. Look for more of his work later as editor of TSA's 2021 members' anthology.

I'm glad to introduce our new tanka prose editor, Liz Lanigan, who opens her section in this issue with a thought-provoking check list of what she looks for in the genre. She comes to us from the robust tanka circles in Canberra, Australia, where she discovered tanka seven years ago with Friday Writers. She says she "wrote a short piece about odd socks that others said was crying out for a tanka to top it off." Soon after that, a weekend spent meeting other tanka poets and learning more about the form at Kathy Kituai's Limestone Tanka Poets got her hooked. Before she retired, Liz "helped people who had not succeeded at school, teaching them about how language works and encouraging them to enjoy reading and writing." For a year, she even coordinated a literacy program in a remote Aboriginal community.

Then there's Michael McClintock. In 2001, he originated the Tanka Café as an "open forum" for members to share tanka "in whatever style they wrote." A vital part of it, he says, was the Member's Choice Award, conceived as a "continuous loop mechanism, to give feedback, commentary, and criticism," complementing his role as Café columnist and host. With each issue, he offers an intriguing new prompt and invites members to comment on their tanka if they wish. His introduction, drawing on these comments, and the Member's Choice essay help create that sense of community in *Ribbons*. Worth mentioning, in 2005, at the start of his five years as TSA President, Michael launched *Ribbons* with the board's help and an'ya as its first editor and printer, to supplement the society's newsletter.

I welcome Mary Ahearn from South Coventry, Pennsylvania, and Ginny Short, from Thousand Palms, California, as proofreaders, an important contribution to the journal, if often unsung. I came to know them and their work as contributors of tanka prose. I also thank TSA President Michael Dylan Welch for his help in many ways, including writing one of the book reviews in this issue.

I'm pleased we can all walk together on this tanka journey.

Hawk Mountain porch
worn hiking boots
abloom with marigolds . . .
finding in retirement
new ways to flourish

—*Susan Weaver*

The Tanka Café

Featured at the Café

With each issue, a "Member's Choice Tanka" will be selected from the previous installment of the "Tanka Café" to receive an honorarium of $25. Monies for the award are provided from the general fund of the Tanka Society of America. All poems appearing in each installment of the "Tanka Café" will be eligible for this recognition.

Each recipient of the "Member's Choice Tanka" award is asked to make the next award selection, along with two or three commended poems from the next set, and to offer a few comments on their choice for the award. In this case, Kathy Kituai has chosen our "Member's Choice Tanka" and commended poems from the "Escapes" set in the Winter 2021 "Tanka Café."

—Michael McClintock

Member's Choice Tanka
Kathy Kituai

I should have known, during as bleak a period as I experienced with illness and setbacks since the beginning of the year, that it was possible something could take me by surprise and fill me with joy. Thanks to James Chessing for being the bearer of that gift by choosing my tanka as Member's Choice. His perception that I learned to give of my best no matter the task in hand by witnessing the way in which my grandfather cared for his bench and tools, was insightful and reassuring.

This wouldn't have been possible without Michael McClintock's never-ending, thought-provoking topics and discussion for Tanka

Café. Nonetheless, the prompt, *escape,* for this issue seemed an immense one to explore. Many poets offered creative ways in which they dealt with it by turning to the beauty of the environment and a love of books for inspiration, strength, and peace, but three tanka stood out to me for their originality.

The first is Giselle Maya's tanka that comes with an invitation to envision birdlife some of us may not be fond of in forests confronted with icy, seasonal conditions, coincidentally at a time when the world is faced with the chilling reality of COVID-19:

> imagine
> an exultation of sparrows
> in a winter forest
> you scatter a handful
> of sunflower seeds

Giselle Maya, St. Martin de Castillon, France

Without warning, when I read "an exultation of sparrows" in the first line of her tanka, I took a deep breath, closed my eyes, and repeated those words aloud just to hear and feel them on my tongue. I recited this phrase throughout the day. A mantra, this is a phrase that doesn't just arrest the mind. It resonates throughout the body.

Then just as unexpectedly, I remembered how house sparrows steal seeds, even as I sew them in my veggie patch. And that in Australia they are an introduced species that destroy native birds' nests, eggs, and nestlings as they compete for nesting spaces. Are they worthy of such adulation? Still, they never kill to eat. Besides, are all breeds of birds as chirpy, family-minded, and friendly as sparrows?

According to Frankie Schembri (*Science,* August 24, 2018), "The house sparrow's friendly behaviour is legendary, with references cropping up in the Bible, early Chinese poetry, and Geoffrey Chaucer's *The Canterbury Tales.*" And now brought to us again in tanka (Japanese poetry), thanks to Giselle.

Do house sparrows differ significantly from those who reside in forests? This is surely so. However, in 2010, as a writer-in-residence in Lochinvar, Scotland, far from family, all that was on my mind was the joy in saving them titbits from dinner plates, and their cheerful ovation when fed.

In lockdown we can do with friends. Some may be closer than thought to be, and not necessarily limited to human beings.

It wasn't just for one phrase alone that I settled on Giselle's tanka as the winner. She is asking us to not only imagine sparrows in a winter forest but to scatter sunflower seed that sustains them. Any poet who sees a positive side to birds many view as pests has my gratitude and respect. How euphoric it could be to look anew at things annoying and menacing, to view them in a different light, and perhaps to applaud them. Could any invitation be timelier than this during COVID-19?

Poetically, the resonance of 's' echoes through Giselle's tanka in *sparrows*, *forest*, *scatter*, *sunflower*, and *seeds*, another reason this tanka is a standout.

I also kept returning to Bob Lucky's tanka — again for the original and intriguing point of view that highlights Giselle's tanka.

the window ajar
to let the darkness out
lockdown fatigue
crossing out words
to free a poem

Bob Lucky, Viana do Castelo, Portugal

It is usual to close a window, sometimes drawing the drapes to keep darkness out. Bob suggests that we open the window and let it escape, quite the opposite point of view. During lockdown many of us discovered that by letting go of a competitive, busy, and stressful way of life–another kind of gloom–isolation came with gifts. Many took up cooking, gardening, spending the morning in pj's, and let the light into their lives with a slower, more satisfying, and healthier way of being. Lockdown fatigue vanished. Cutting back on business can release us into a more abundant lifestyle.

For me, it is normal to escape into poetry pre-dawn with a notebook on my lap, curtains pulled aside to watch sunrise, a cat curled up nearby, and create new poetry and prose while "bright-brain" is in place after a restful night's sleep or edit what I wrote the morning before, as I'm doing right now. Crossing out words, as Bob suggests, is a way to let a poem say what it came to say. Less is more, as we know, particularly in tanka. How challenging but sustaining it is to write simply with as few words as possible, but isn't this the very thing that makes writing tanka attractive?

It takes a master poet to say something as profound as this. Bob, a poet I've admired for years, conveys this message. The parallel of releasing darkness and fostering the light by omitting words in a poem is related in a way not usually expressed; the pivot, "lockdown fatigue," is relevant to both issues.

Not unlike Bob's tanka, Ken Slaughter's tanka suggests that the way to find peace is through facing the pain and reflecting on it instead of seeking the means to distract ourselves.

a tree
with a gash in its trunk—
at last in the shade
I make peace
with my wounds

Ken Slaughter, Worcester, MA

This demands mindfulness, takes time and effort. Ken took the time to search for a comforting place in which to take stock of what caused him harm and expresses this well in the third line—"at last in the shade." This implies that time must have passed before he found it. This is a line I also see as a pivot, even though there is a dash after "trunk." Trees have no choice to do anything other than continue to grow. Is it pressing this point too far to suggest they heal in the process? I choose to think they are also at peace and embrace the fact that trees are "at last in the shade," as well.

I have watched a Ribbon Bark tree, for twenty years in the park close to my back fence, twist and bend with every gust of wind during storms. It cannot escape where it's planted, and to witness this behaviour, see it survive and grow, have encouraged me to go with the flow, accept whatever comes my way as much as I can. Trees are anything other than passive. We can be brought down by emotional storms, be swept away with passion, and rail against lacerations; or we can face problems, resist the urge to escape what seems to want to wound. These are some of the thoughts Ken's tanka instills in me. I also keep in mind that there are times it's wise to run away.

A tree hugger from way back, I view trees as some of our greatest teachers and have singled this tanka out for an honourable mention, along with Bob Lucky's, because of the unique insight both offer.

Tanka Café: Spring Love

First, welcome to our new *Ribbons* editor, Susan Weaver, with whom we move forward in our study and enjoyment of contemporary tanka. Susan brings a wide knowledge of the literature and the poetics involved, combined with a fine sense of organization, coordination of all the parts that make *Ribbons* what it is, and a pragmatic, clear vision of how best to explore and present the fruits our contributors bring to the table. Yielding our best work, through thousands of interactions that go into making each issue, is our goal and overriding purpose.

Our present set on "Spring Love" offers an abundance of good results. I'm especially grateful for Joy McCall's expansive reflections on the theme. "There are so many, many things I could write about spring love," McCall explains. "I focus mostly about my sense of being part of the whole, when the sap is rising and the leaves are green, and there's blossom and bees and butterflies. When the leaves fall and the snows come, it is much the same feeling within me. But that's all about nature, and you asked for human love, and there too there's so much I could write. The poem I am submitting is what came. . . Growing old with my soul mate, Andy, I realize we are very lucky. The vicar cares for everyone in the parish, no matter what, even those of us who are not 'religious'—heathen or Christian or Sufi. Hindu or Muslim or Jew, pagan or rich or poor, crooks or worshippers. He judges no one and loves them all. He welcomes those with mental illness to come to garden with him in the church yard. He welcomes the homeless and feeds and clothes them. He runs errands for shut-ins. He asks all kinds, young and old, to be part of the church services. The congregation grows! To me, any kind of God looking down would be pleased, especially the One he loves."

Like the poets of previous ages and times, the contributors to this set appear to interact with the world by enfolding and transforming its life and the "stuff" of its material into a sense of self. Michele L. Harvey comments, "To me spring is irrepressible and beguiling, no matter one's age or situation. It's a tide's tug; a tsunami of love, washing over all that's alive. As I've gotten older, I've come to know it's not personal, but all pervasive like the sun, rejecting none. Can't you feel it? I can."

Sheila Sondik describes how daffodils transform into something else. "This year, my spring love object is the season itself. I feel almost ecstatic on my daily walks, thanks to the newborn flowers and foliage and the strong, ever-more cheerful sunlight. The daffodils started it all. 'Davening' is Yiddish for praying, and for me evokes the daffodils as an image of standing, swaying worshippers."

John Quinnett connects the season to key events in his life, and to a kind of resurrection. "I met my first wife in San Francisco in 1968, the year after the 'Summer of Love.' If there was ever a 'flower child,' it was Marita. When we moved to the Great Smokies in North Carolina, the two of us did a lot of hiking in the mountains together, especially in the springtime, to enjoy the wildflowers. She died suddenly in April, 1977, when the floral beauty of the Smokies can take your breath away. And it's in April, every year since, that I go hiking with her again."

Teri White Carns leaves us with a last word about kites. "Kites remind me of the Prince Charming marionette that my mother made for me when I was about nine or ten years old. I could never manage to get the marionette to do what I wanted. It was always a tangled heap, mocking my incompetence. At some time in my early thirties, I realized that Prince Charming could symbolize all of my failed relationships. I cut the strings away from Mr. Charming, and did much better thereafter."

—Michael McClintock

can love be holy?
i am your
eucharist
pure white
& edible

Pamela A. Babusci

kanji for holy

the young vicar
lays pound coins and cake
and primrose pots
and the sign of peace
at any opening door

Joy McCall, Norwich, UK

purple ice plant
carpets our shoreline
in the spring —
there under a canopy
we renew our wedding vows

Neal Whitman, Pacific Grove, CA

where the mountain stream
stops rushing, and pools
into a pool
        —finding the words
I want to say to you

Robert Kusch, Piscataway, NJ

alone for weeks
I open the cottage window
to spring sunshine
two teenagers French-kissing
with masks under their chins

Chen-ou Liu, Ajax, ON, Canada

spring blossoms
their fragrance
so bewitching
my moist lips
savor her elixir

John Budan, Newburg, OR

the late spring
light in my courtyard
suffused
with golden roses . . .
"sheltering in place"

Amelia Fielden, Belconnen, ACT, Australia

certain beauty
no other time of year . . .
knowing this
feeling and seeing this
i love my life

Pat Geyer, East Brunswick, NJ

I just asked
about a symbol
for 5th Anniversary
strong roots
and enduring

Carmen Sterba, University Place, WA

a wildfire
lit with a cigarette
spring love
i fall
for the bad boy

Marilyn Ashbaugh, Edwardsburg, MI

April mist
rising from the lagoon—
so carelessly
we drifted together
into separate winters

Ruth Holzer, Herndon, VA

the days
lengthening in spring
I linger in bed
for what's leftover
of my dream of you

Jackie Chou, Pico Rivera, CA

vaccination spring
we love you Giancarlo
our daughter says *he replays*
talks to you like you're here
we count the days

Kath Abela Wilson, Pasadena, CA

a fourth year
in the same fork
of a blooming apple tree
a robin's nest . . .
spring renewal

James B. Peters, Cottontown, TN

she pines for the boy
with the funny crooked grin
who kissed her at camp
as the last snow of winter
disappears into her dreams

Michael H. Lester, Los Angeles, CA

sun and water
shimmer on contact
opening the camp
the boy across the lake
her first real kiss

Ignatius Fay, Sudbury, ON, Canada

swish swish
of the neighbor's broom
an early spring
and the girl next door
arrives home with a new lover

Christopher Costable, Valrico, FL

spring fragrance
a nod for brittle bones
following the trail . . .
this need to find the carved heart
and our tree still standing

Tish Davis, Concord Twp., OH

a spring breeze
lifting my hair . . .
the touch
of your fingertips
centers my desire

Rebecca Drouilhet, Picayune, MS

purple iris
wakened by the sun's caress
exuberant
my new love emboldened
on this fine spring day

David Lee Hill, Bakersfield, CA

spring bamboo—
a single night spent
without you
I grind my tears deep
into the ink stone

an'ya, Florence, OR

the constant change
of spring weather
the verve
of days to come
in her eyes

Mike Montreuil, Ottawa, ON, Canada

digging in warm soil
helping out in her garden
feels like spring again
although our flowers
have gone off to college

Charles Harmon, Los Angeles, CA

cherry blossom
the first poem
written today
about the death of love
hopefully the last

Steve Black, Reading, United Kingdom

blossoms and new grass
the exuberant honking
of returning geese
all this is mine to accept
if I hold out my hands

Adelaide B. Shaw, Somers, NY

spring rain
refilling
the empty well
not knowing the depths
of my desire

Bryan Rickert, Belleville, IL

forever love
pledged in the playground
with a ring
belonging to his mother . . .
mum makes me give it back

Liz Lanigan, Canberra, Australia

eight fuzzy goslings
hidden and kept warm and safe
by mom on the nest
and by dad nearby
patrolling their pond

Elinor Pihl Huggett, Lakeville, IN

Spring love
or merely lust?
Heaven or Hell?
Will it freeze over
by winter?

Bob Loomis, Concord, CA

winter thaw
gives way to spring
a mother cat
five fluffy kittens
i choose the pick of the litter

Taura Scott, Duarte, CA

although
she no longer knows him
he visits each week
clean shirt, polished shoes
and today . . . daffodils

Catherine Smith, Sydney, Australia

springing awake
beside my new love
I postpone
advancing the clock
this time will be better spent

Joyce S. Greene, Poughkeepsie, NY

both of us relieved
we made it to this side
of the pandemic—
falling back in love
with spring's soft greening

Mary Kendall, Chapel Hill, NC

two wrens
build a log cabin
together
spring love blinds them
to death's jaws below

Ray Spitzenberger, East Bernard, TX

a robin pair
worming on the grass
surrender
themselves to feeding well
the hatchlings in their nest

Paul Cordeiro, Dartmouth, MA

spring day—
a bluejay's whisper song
makes me pause . . .
don't we all want
someone to love

Susan Burch, Hagerstown, MD

How many poems
I have to compose this spring
for you, my dearest,
to make you see with eyes of
love my soul naked for you

Ricardo J. Bogaert-Alvarez, Denver, CO

gathering daisies
in their last spring
together . . .
he strokes her palm
before softly kissing it

Carol Raisfeld, Atlantic Beach, NY

a red rose
how grandmother blushes
when she sees him
after all these years his voice
the longest in her mind

Xenia Tran, Nairn, Scotland

LGBTQI+
so many words to describe
the love
that blooms all around me—
I just need someone who cares

Keitha Keyes, Sydney, NSW, Australia

first love
he gives me a bracelet
of clover
fourteen years old
a dream takes flight

Barbara Tate, Winchester, TN

the spring of my life
is bubbling, spilling over
with lots of things
to say, see and do
who says 80 is old

Genie Nakano, Gardena, CA

Romeo and Juliet
touch millions
on screen and stage
in real life
how many would act like them?

Nu Quang, Seattle, WA

blackbirds complain
ice in the birdbath
cold nights, warm days
he always liked spring
I never liked the mud

Lenore English, Grand Rapids, MI

pure love . . .
the depths my soul knows
add a sojourn
into an earthy body
with a tiny twist of lust

Judith Morrison Schallberger, San Jose, CA

in next-door's garden
rows of strawberries blushing
crimson-warm
is it theft to taste
just one for ripeness?

Michelle Brock, Queanbeyan, NSW, Australia

at eighty I love
every thing and one
but it's another love I crave–
Springtime, knock me over
with your full blown coup d'amour

Margaret Van Every, Ajijic, Jalisco, Mexico

spring morning
rawness
of drizzle . . .
warmth of the hearth
and her arms

David F. Noble, Charlottesville, VA

here you are again,
passing in the window,
your long hair
shining in the sunlight
like waters in a brook

Michael McClintock, Clovis, CA

if a tear spills
from your lover's eye
save it for spring
to float you beyond this life
before summer's blossoms fall

Linda Jeannette Ward, Coinjock, NC

Stack of opera CDs
I put on my Goth clothes
and listen again
to songs of youth, songs of love
songs of betrayal and revenge

J. Zimmerman, Santa Cruz, CA

this side of life
with blue shadows and ebb tide . . .
but spring
with open invitation
calls everyone to the dance

Michele L. Harvey, Hamilton, NY

skipping stones
across calm, clear water . . .
my heart
beats so much faster
as I'm falling into love

Susan Constable, Parksville, BC, Canada

to line her nest, a merganser
plucks down from her breast—
it took far too long
for me to appreciate the sacrifice
my mother made for us

Sally Biggar, Topsham, ME

       the smell
       of blossoms in the air
       even
       the trees know
       our secret

       Marilyn Fleming, Pewaukee, WI

spring
a stack of the pink
kimonos
   untouched
unbloomed

Barun Saha, Bangalore, India

       I gave up everything
       for his desire
       but spring
       doubt sprouting
       with the daffodils

       Susan Weaver, Allentown, PA

one Easter morning
two glanced as they passed
without a word
a fire started that burns yet
beyond the grave

Michael Flanagan, Woodburg, MN

> he mounts her
> one, two, three, four times
> then flies away
> to gather twigs and grasses
> for their nest
>
> *Margaret Chula, Portland, OR*

you were a neighbor
smiling with uncertainty
six feet away
now, spring a soft white flurry
we lean into new bliss

Linda Conroy, Bellingham, WA

> Mary said
> see this clematis
> i nurtured so long
> this spring
> it's come to bloom
>
> *David Chandler, Chicago, IL*

tiny yellow balls
on the nearby plum tree
baby plums
no matter what
how I love this world

Jeanne Lupton, Berkeley, CA

spring love
in the autumn of life
is not only blind
but increasingly deaf
and not at all sure-footed

Elaine Riddell, Hamilton, NZ

spring fever
those Dionysian days
spent by the river
leaning back on the cool grasses
taking it all in

Mary Frederick Ahearn, South Coventry, PA

first-class
on the eastbound night train
I envision
my war-hero boyfriend
waiting for me back at track three

Roberta Beach Jacobson, Indianola, IA

poppy field
an undulating
frenzy of orange
passion this hot
won't be subdued

Ina Scott, Lancaster, CA

a Wodehouse
with your name scrawled
in the bookcase . . .
all that I have to remember
a brief holiday

Madhuri Pillai, Melbourne, Australia

first breath of warmth
pear blossoms suddenly
everywhere
my will to continue
slowly returning

Carmel Summers, Canberra, Australia

is it still there?
I cannot see it on
your face
shadowed now
by dementia

Erika Wilk, Pasadena, CA

my new love and I
two thousand miles quarantined—
a year of sweet talk
only by phone and zoom calls
till springtime vaccine allows

Vince Gotera, Waterloo, IA

I've heard that angels
　elbow each other
on the head of a pin—
but here it's spring when lovers
　sprawl on park lawns

Victor Ortiz, Bellingham, WA

until he met her
he'd never liked hiking
sunshine
in a meadow of color
a kiss

Johnnie Johnson Hafernik, San Francisco, CA

he brings me
bright yellow pansies
in a Limoges teacup
I trace the cracks
mended with gold

Dru Philippou, Taos, NM

false spring
like old love letters torn up
betrayed
still I plant these seeds deep
forgiveness overflowing

Marjorie Buettner, Chisago City, MN

the scent
of orange blossoms
floats
from the orchard . . .
the sky fills with stars

Beatrice Yell, Sydney, Australia

the orchid
hasn't died yet—
spring breeze
the chile peppers
getting redder and redder

Bob Lucky, Viana do Castelo, Portugal

wildflowers
fill the meadow
the thrill
of our day together
can be seen in my stained dress

Pris Campbell, Lake Worth, FL

raindrops at dusk
the soft palette
opening the door
to an aria
of birdsong

Joanna Ashwell, Barnard Castle, UK

the springtime ritual
of another deep cleaning
behind the heavy desk
a long lost letter
from a long lost love

Helen Ogden, Pacific Grove, CA

in the silence
of moonlight
we draw
closer together
first date

Dawn Bruce, St. Leonards, NSW, Australia

sky dance—
two hawks calling
each to each
soar together on the wind
as if the world were new

Jenny Ward Angyal, Gibsonville, NC

Canadian-grown
flats of blooming pansies
wait for warmer beds . . .
after April showers,
we shimmy beneath sheets

Mary Singer, Manchester, NH

        periwinkle crocuses
        bloomed on our first date
        as we ate lunch
        in a little Italian restaurant
        you tiptoed into my heart

        Mary Davila, Buffalo, NY

fifty-two years
into our marriage
every season
more deeply filled
with spring

Edward Rielly, Westbrook, ME

        in our park
        of rose-tinted memories
        searching
        for first love's eyes
        in every gnarled face

        Carole Harrison, Jamberoo, NSW, Australia

on the doorstep
too much
too little
too late—
yellow roses

Cynthia Anderson, Yucca Valley, CA

on a pathway
of petals and wind
we stroll
between flowering trees
toward new daydreams

Margarita Engle, Clovis, CA

hand in hand
hiking this mountain trail
in April as ever . . .
I always promised
to bring you flowers

John Quinnett, Bryson City, NC

vernal equinox
balance shifting to the light
emerging
sprouts of love and kindness
hope for this small planet

Robert Erlandson, Birmingham, MI

the setter practices
with the young coach
try as she might
her fingers can't quell
the spinning of her heart

James Chessing, San Ramon, CA

longer days
and shorter skirts
with the flow
how the spring flowers
do open up

Robert B. McNeill, Winchester, VA

blooming forsythia
the birds and the bees
my wife and I
all up and about
this sunny day

Michael Ketchek, Rochester, NY

how many
springs since
my love
passed away
cherry blossom rain

Mariko Kitakubo, Tokyo, Japan

banquets of bees
gathering honey of words
from this flower
and that flower
ceaselessly linger

Aya Yuhki, Tokyo, Japan

it's now late fall
but I remember the spring
when the air was bright
your crooked smile
captured my heart

Laurance Sumners, Lufkin, TX

writing night
with all this spring jazz
and dim lights
I want to hold you
skin to skin

Lenard D. Moore, Raleigh, NC

the moon was full
on our first date
driving home
I saw the sunrise
for the first time in years

Gregory Longenecker, Pasadena, CA

together in their winter years
each caring for the other
both sad and smiling
sitting and remembering
spring love blooming in the snow

Trilla Pando, Houston, TX

I call him Shiki
a little black cat
who has taken refuge
in my house
I give him my spring love

Giselle Maya, St. Martin de Castillon, France

spring was eternal
before the metronome
began keeping time
young men dreamed dreams
old men saw visions

John Tehan, Cape Cod, MA

a roe deer leaps
across our dappled path
and into Rumi . . .
*behind the words
is the voice of the heart*

Claire Everett, North Yorkshire, England

spring moon
in silence I reach
for your hand
it should be more complex
　　　　this love poem

celia stuart-powles, Tulsa, OK

　　　　in the soft light
　　　　under the swollen buds
　　　　of the magnolia
　　　　the cardinal gently feeds his mate
　　　　from the pile of scattered seeds

　　　　Sharon Hammer Baker, Findlay, OH

new ritual
a daily lockdown walk
around the lake
as the silvery fog lifts
the mating dance of swans

Iliyana Stoyanova, St Albans, UK

　　　　when she dies
　　　　he decides
　　　　to follow
　　　　then the rain
　　　　then flowers

　　　　LeRoy Gorman, Napanee, ON, Canada

silent prayer
for Fukushima victims
under cherry blossoms—
ten years have already passed
still unable to go home

Mari Konno, Fukui, Japan

        spring love
        how she still butters
        his toast
        as if one day
        he'll remember

        Peter Jastermsky, Morongo Valley, CA

spring arrives
as love's gaze lingers
and the heart's
wild geese take flight
into the dazzling sun

William Scott Galasso, Laguna Woods, CA

        I want to embrace
        this fever dream of spring
        daffodils howling
        as dandelions shout
        look at me! and I do

        Marilyn Hazelton, Allentown, PA

new grave
where our old dog
finally rests
a cool morning rain
darkens the soil

Michael Blaine, Seaford, DE

a flare
of forsythia
boldly aglow —
could tonight
be the night?

Elizabeth Martens, Philadelphia, PA

Another spring
she welcomes the rebirth
of old friends
digs gently around their roots
tells them about her winter

Joanne Watcyn-Jones, Sydney, Australia

tenderness
of the first
waking moment
just before the day
brightens for you

Natalia L Rudychev, New York, NY

loving the kite's swoops
more than the man behind the string
no desire to be tied
to Prince Charming, or a kite—
breaking the silver threads now

Teri White Carns, Anchorage, AL

there's a host
of golden daffodils
davening
psalms of gratitude
outside our front door

Sheila Sondik, Bellingham, WA

late in life
mine and his
yet every day on our walk
my little dog leads the way
without words

Tom Clausen, Ithaca, NY

a few small kicks
from under the table
that convey interest in me
a small kick back
that the teacher doesn't see

Patricia Wakimoto, Gardena, CA

spring fever
a box of old love
letters opened
fifty years too late
for my responses

an'ya

Next Tanka Café Theme: The Inner Life

Deadline: August 31, 2021

The Tanka Society of America invites members to submit one original, unpublished tanka for each installment of "The Tanka Café" appearing in this journal.

Write a tanka drawn from your inner life, however you may conceive or experience it. Can you capture and share its essence in a few words? Is it peaceful or stormy? Restless or placid? Underneath the layers, is there a deeper, more solid foundation, or is it molten and transitory? Is it an empty room, a monkey cage, or an ocean? Please note that poems submitted to Tanka Café are considered "published" when they appear; thus you need to be cautious about submitting them to other venues, especially to contests, which may require that all work submitted be unpublished and/or not under consideration elsewhere. Generally, restrictions are few and almost any treatment will be acceptable. The overall challenge will be to submit one's very best effort. All poems will be read for depth and "layering" of meaning, substance, thematic content, etc.

About eighty of the best poems fitting the theme will appear in the next installment of the Tanka Café. Please understand that any note accompanying your submission may also be considered for publication, in whole or in part. Send your submission to Michael McClintock via email to mchlmcclintock@aol.com with the subject heading "Tanka Café" (be certain to use the subject heading, please), or via mail to Michael McClintock, 1830 N. Bush Avenue, Clovis, CA 93619 (no SASE necessary). Be sure to include your full name as you wish it to appear beneath the poem, followed by your town or city of residence and its location (state, province, and country): see examples throughout this journal. The in-hand deadline is August 31, 2021.

—Michael McClintock

Selected Tanka

spring came
when we weren't looking
he pulls weeds
another season blooms
as we grow old together

Lenore English, Grand Rapids, MI

another Philly Friday
all are enchanted by
a small man who holds
forsythia and pussy willows
on the Septa Bus

Carmen Sterba, Seattle, WA

the pond warming up
squirming on the surface
new life—
for my ninth birthday
a *real* microscope

Neal Whitman, Pacific Grove, CA

in the silence
of the gray dawn
floating
are numerous white buds—
Magnolia chandelier

Mari Konno, Fukui, Japan

spring breeze
a floral breath
sings memories
of grandma's
perfume

Sean MicKael Wilson, Ionia, MI

saguaro cactus
bloom two months before their time
sonoran desert
calls down thunder, lightning, rain
for the miracle of fruit

Barbara Robidoux, Santa Fe, NM

cusp of spring
in the pour of morning tea
my hearing loss
   taken for granted
   each day's musicality

Judith Morrison Schallberger, San Jose, CA

garden party
bumble bees humming
in the Matisse roses
I arrange the tea set
and the goldfish bowl

carolyne rohrig, Freemont, CA

how the light flatters
her sheer dress
and all the secrets
she doesn't know
she's sharing

Peter Jastermsky, Morongo, CA

sunrise
a sparrow takes flight . . .
dew drops
in a shower of light
spring from the branch

Elaine Riddell, Hamilton, New Zealand

seed and sun
in the field I found
my bloom
among wildflowers . . .
this someday soil

Kat Lehmann, Guilford, CT

lingering dusk
one lone cicada singing
accompanied
by children laughing
playing tag in the street

Robert Erlandson, Birmingham, MI

soft clicking
of a bamboo wind chime
rose petals scattered
across the pavement
from the passing storm

Sharon Hammer Baker, Findlay, OH

cleaning the yard
after the storm
turns into pruning
the rosemary . . .
grilled salmon

Gideon Young, Chapel Hill, NC

forgotten heat—
echoing
across the valley
the harsh cries
of peacocks

Cynthia Anderson, Yucca Valley, CA

Independence Day
pierces my soul—
thunderstorms
lash across the road
and hills

Oscar Montes, Detroit, MI

it matters little
if you call it the firefly
and I say glow worm
the light was alive yesterday
today it is no more

Lakshmi Iyer, Trivandrum, Kerala, India

wild geese
their honks outstretched
across sky's grey
not such a small thing
this sureness of flight

Louisa Howerow, Ontario, Canada

First time around
the October lake
the couple walked hand in hand
but this time around
she's far ahead

Brook Zelcer, Cresskill, NJ

autumn's grey sea
its sturdy roll and rumble
so like dull highway din
I think of constancy
essential for our lives

Linda Conroy, Bellingham, WA

with its antlers
the buck engraves a billet-doux
on the smooth-barked beech
a lusty calligraphy
that needs no interpreter

Burl N. Corbett, St. Petersburg, FL

in the front yard
on the top limb
of the crepe myrtle
a winter bright cardinal
against the gray sky

James B. Peters, Cottontown, TN

overnight
the rain turns to ice . . .
I slide
through another
bad dream

Dave Read, Calgary, Alberta, Canada

seeking refuge
under a misty bridge
of nothingness
when the wind exposes
my primordial bones

Hifsa Ashraf, Rawalpindi, Pakistan

a sable goddess
baring her shoulder
this winter night
I feel the dark moon rise
over a world of men

Claire Everett, North Yorkshire, England

three days
since the latest
heavy snowfall
still no footprints
lead to my door

Ignatius Fay, Sudbury, ON, Canada

so alone
I drift through
the Milky Way
a cosmic piece
of dust

Susan Burch, Hagerstown, MD

painful music
wafts through the room
familiar sound
of blues
in the darkness

Mel Goldberg, Laredo, TX

deepening ruts
in the driveway . . .
another
FedEx package
by the garage

Elinor Pihl Huggett, Lakeville, IN

Sunday oozes
with silence and solitude
through parted curtains
sun and I squint
to greet each other

Madhuri Pillai, Melbourne, Australia

on the trail
two unmasked men
smirk
at our face masks—
the sunlight briefly dims

Sheila Sondik, Bellingham, WA

all is quiet
in winter's lockdown
nature gives
and we gratefully greet
the deer near our windows

Xenia Tran, Nairn, Scotland

pandemic lingers . . .
what empty black bleachers
in the gym
as the game goes on
this rainy night

Lenard D. Moore, Raleigh, NC

out of the attic
hardback forties novels
on love, murder, war—
sunburnt pages of the month
held in a workman's hands

Paul Cordeiro, Dartmouth, MA

picking the berries
in my own backyard . . .
April rain
the sweetness of nature
ignoring a lockdown

C. William Hinderliter, Phoenix, AZ

Children play hopscotch
moving forward square to square,
now in the moment.
There are many numbered days
and a long journey ahead.

Lucia Haase, Spring Valley, IL

lockdown afternoon
a little girl sorts
the colours
of the buttons
in a biscuit tin

Patricia Prime, Auckland, New Zealand

tv shelved . . .
tonight on line
live chat
with a French poet
in London's lockdown

Beatrice Yell, Belrose, Sydney, Australia

scrambled legs
hang over the sofa's edge
as she watches tv
with me—her great dane head
in my lap for ear rubs

Claire Vogel Camargo, Austin, TX

night lingers
sleepily in the bedclothes
our furry heart
pads into the room
meowing for breakfast

Maxianne Berger, Outremont, Quebec, Canada

smothered
in kisses
my dear cat
looks at me
with nonchalance

Tom Clausen, Ithaca, NY

piano recital
by our new kitten
at midnight
a tuneless piece
but a nice light touch

Catherine Smith, Sydney, Australia

chin on paw
she opens one eye
and winks
reassured
she continues her nap

celia stuart-powles, Tulsa, OK

down from the house
the old tabby's grave
in the piney woods
a bobcat's prints melt
in the last of the snow

Mary Frederick Ahearn, South Coventry, PA

a collection
of beach glass
and empty shells
recalling the things that time
and tides have left behind

Rick Jackofsky, Rocky Point, NY

reading
her old letters in bed
nostalgia
the fragrance of the past
tangled in the sheets

Bob Lucky, Viana do Castelo, Portugal

I'm clearing out
all of her clothes
leaving behind
a faint lavender fragrance
an angry jangle of hangers

Ruth Holzer, Herndon, VA

rain
falling on itself
puddles form
memories
of a long life

Maryalicia Post, Dublin, Ireland

grandma appeared as
the star in a foreign film
but I didn't know
how to read until after
the final credits

Katherine Shehadeh, Miami, FL

she quietly describes
a childhood trauma—
in the waning light
shadows of roses
waver on the wall

Ce Rosenow, Eugene, OR

like water
racing over stones
in mountain streams
how we spent our youth
an untamed wilderness in time

David Lee Hill, Bakersfield, CA

wooden shoes
on a red tile hearth—
memories
leap like goblin flames
fleeing the winter dusk

Jenny Ward Angyal, Gibsonville, NC

plucking out
another white hair
I look out the window
at forget-me-nots
bluer than last year

Chen-ou Liu, Ajax, ON, Canada

respite
pulling me out of myself
cherry blossoms
scatter
troubled wind

Thomas Lyon Freeland, Edmonton, AB, Canada

cloud avalanche
a rare event in Nepal,
descends, obscures
mountains and lake
Sherpas' eyes dance

William Scott Galasso, Laguna Woods, CA

climbing Mount Baldy
hauling a sixty-pound backpack,
two sons,
two stents,
and nitro in my pocket

Juan DePascuale, Gambier, OH

Toscana—
how does that rainbow
over the fields
look to the eyes of pigeons
perched on the spire

Aya Yuhki, Tokyo, Japan

a night free of stars
the moon full and unashamed
a moment distilled
sake reflects this purity
only to be drunk away

George Camile-Perkins, Golts, MD

English woodland
my New World fiancé
calls it a rain forest
the ferns and beech trees
where Wordsworth walked

J. Zimmerman, Santa Cruz, CA

"has the bus come?"
lacking the words
for yes or no
I wipe the bench
so she can sit

Kristyn Blessing, Calumet, MI

when I speak
Japanese to her
she can hear
the sound of chopsticks
click, clack, click

Anne Curran, Hamilton, New Zealand

at high tea
we're asked to choose from
summer, chai, rose pearl . . .
names heard but not tasted
take on a flavour

Margaret Owen Ruckert, Sydney, Australia

low winter sun
Anne Frank's words linger over
the West Bank Wall
silently we share
a group hug

Iliyana Stoyanova, St Albans, UK

doesn't matter
how I measure
six feet or two metres
it's still a journey
across Antarctica

LeRoy Gorman, Napanee, ON, Canada

at belmont that night
the lights inside our train failed
screen zombie faces
lit up like so many
floating skin-covered lanterns

J Shannon Swan, Sudbury, MA

on the train
she styles her self
curling her lashes
from Strathfield
to Redfern

Anne Benjamin, Toongabbie, NSW, Australia

a rainy Thursday
waiting for my clothes to dry
in the laundry room
at Strawberry Creek Lodge
happy for no reason

Jeanne Lupton, Berkeley, CA

near dark
on the C & O Canal
the bats dart
from their cave
on the hillside

Sarah Ockrim, Salem, VA

stark lights
glitter like roman candles
on the harbour
my arm around her
we sit and pretend

Martin Grenfell, Bristol, Somerset, England

restless sea
disappearing
reappearing
the sea otter
in the surf

Helen Ogden, Pacific Grove, CA

you
the setting sun
folded in waves
return to me
on seagull wings

Marilyn Ashbaugh, Edwardsburg, MI

half moon
through streams of cloud
flowing
wisps of silvery hair
a mother-of-pearl comb

Mira Walker, Canberra, Australia

old couple
getting married
two rings
her dress and his suit
from the thrift boutique

Hazel Hall, Aranda ACT, Australia

white heron
meets its shadow
on the lake
my hand was made to fit
inside your palm

Natalia L Rudychev, New York, NY

the evergreen
and the deciduous
compare their deep wounds
arrows plunged into heartwood
the mystery of spring love

Janice S. Garey, Decatur, GA

young lovers
on a bench in the park
oblivious . . .
the way we were
when you loved me

Carol Raisfeld, Atlantic Beach, NY

full-bodied
a hint of cinnamon
and mango . . .
my latin lover
lingers on the palate

Liz Lanigan, Canberra, Australia

fine strands
of hair woven
into a nest . . .
we can never know all
the lives we touch

Michele L. Harvey, Hamilton, NY

a white swan
drifts on dark foam
the barista smiles—
my pleasure in her art
an offering we share

Joanne Watcyn-Jones, Sydney, Australia

the waitress's eyes
follow the couple
to the street
a cold cup of tea
on the table

Jon Hare, Falmouth, MA

ghost winds—
haunted by the thought
of our parting
and the words you spoke
that might be true

Gregory Longenecker, Pasadena, CA

the moon
suspended in blood sunset
almost impossible
the idea you'd want to kill me
amid whispered endearments

Ken Anderson, Victoria, Australia

nearing midnight
echo of footsteps
through empty rooms
I'm not safe here
anymore

Barbara Tate, Winchester, TN

only a woman
inside the man
begs forgiveness
after the quarrel
I serve her tea

John Budan, Newburg, OR

I see her too much
"not enough" you may argue
but I can't take it
each time we cross our paths
my heart breaks a little more

Hugh Allison, London, England

in this quicksand
of night, my confidences sink
even time's embrace
does not free me from
our parallel paths

Richa Sharma, Ghaziabad, Uttar Pradesh, India

A sudden snow in May
breaks the cherry tree's limbs
and I realize
that I am strong enough
to leave him for good

Kathleen Caster Mace, Niwot, CO

crossing
the river at night
smooth water worn pebbles
on bare toes curling
to trust them

JeanMarie Gossard, Boston, MA

blinding rain—
I will not let the river
take me back again
clinging to the leeward side
of the rock

Bill Pauly, Asbury, IA
Julie Schwerin, Greendale, WI

forgotten
out of reach—
your face, your name
yet even still
a ripple on the tide

Joanna Ashwell, Barnard Castle, UK

after hopping
from one bed to another
she discovers
the love of her life . . .
an accidental child

Susan Constable, Parksville, BC, Canada

the rustle
of the forest
covers the silence
my son finds
more porcini than me

Pasquale Asprea, Genoa, Italy

carrying children
thin brown parents
wade the river
in this Chicago
mural wall

David Chandler, Chicago, IL

the little girl
in the wheelbarrow race
changing the world
one stereotype
at a time

Carole Harrison, Jamberoo, NSW, Australia

by the roadside
a teddy bear
holds a wilted flower
my daughter
wants to rescue it

Mark Teaford, Napa, CA

the hatchling
dead below the nest
these thoughts
about how my life
was never meant to be

Bryan Rickert, Belleville, IL

the vine crept in
through the window
wrapped itself
around me
like you never did

Taura Scott, Duarte, CA

two squirrels
mating on my deck
my neighbor
tells me more
than I want to know

Seren Fargo, Bellingham, WA

worm-holes
in this season's tomatoes . . .
if I remove
blemish after blemish,
what will be left of love

Kathy Kituai, Canberra, Australia

what happens
to a reputation
gone bad
the scent of mildew
on my sweater

Jackie Chou, Pico Rivera, CA

she studies herself
wearing her late sister's dress
when the reflection
in the mirror reminds her:
You are the smart one

James Chessing, San Ramon, CA

No one says a word
about my dress
therefore I
remain quiet
the rest of the night

Alexis Rotella, Greensboro, NC

morning tide
washes debris away—
why do you
find it so hard
to let things go

Mary Kendall, Chapel Hill, NC

honoring your wish
I set your poems ablaze
carbonized words fly
like the second hand's shadow
a black fluttering of time

Linda Jeannette Ward, Coinjock, NC

summer rain
glazes the window
how hard it is
to find the right words
for your obituary

Kathryn J. Stevens, Cary, NC

monitor pads
pasted to his chest
as an IV drips . . .
yet outside his window
a sparrow's song . . .

Mary Davila, Buffalo, NY

faceless white-coats
swarm my gurney
trying to decide . . .
the power
of Nero's thumb

Elliott Simons, Southborough, MA

they say a miss
is as good as a mile
but my brushes with death
do not paint
a pretty picture

Charles Harmon, Los Angeles, CA

your bag came home
yarn, needles . . . a few squares
of bright little flowers
each knot just so
until the last

Michael Flanagan, Woodburg, MN

tears for lost brothers
wash coal dust
from cheeks . . .
laments slide
from steel guitars

David F. Noble, Charlottesville, VA

the clock blinks
draining a whisper
of my sand
stretching the shadow
at my feet

William Hart, Montrose, CA

its smell fills my house
smoldering bones of strangers
I hear a trumpet call
mariachi for the dead
I shut the window and cry

Pam Momoko Yan, Los Angeles, CA

my dead mother
visits me in dream
as if she were here
tigerlily pollen
on my granddaughter's nose

Marjorie Buettner, Chisago City, MN

curves
of the marble nude
pitted by rain—
my dead mother's words:
Seize the day!

Ryland Shengzhi Li, Arlington, VA

soul migration—
remembering you
as morning birds sing
a flock disappears
into a deep purple sky

Jacob Salzer, Vancouver, WA

through my grief
your presence condensing
to memory
a yellow sawdust shadow
where the alder lay

Aron Rothstein, Toledo, OR

I walk
through a birch forest . . .
out of mist
the long echoes
of a woodpecker's knock

David He, Zhuanglang, China

a splash
at the river's edge
willfully
the fish leaps
into the heron's mouth

Marilyn Fleming, Pewaukee, WI

she curses
the home help
the footballs
she never threw back
littering the yard

Steve Black, Reading, United Kingdom

every time I think
I have a handle on things . . .
a door's left unlocked
a window's left ajar
my skirt's up in back

Marcyn Del Clements, Clairemont, CA

grand opening
of a fine downtown bistro
we sample from
the Camembert and olive platter
as the server spills our wine

Roberta Beach Jacobson, Indianola, IA

today the thrush again
pecks at my window
cocks its head like the RCA dog
wanting answers
of which I have none

Margaret Van Every, Ajijic, Jalisco, Mexico

if I want
my dying to mean something
have I fallen short
of enlightenment
on all three marks of existence?

Sandra Renew, Canberra, Australia

of what consequence
is my life
a train
rumbles by on
its midnight run

Marje A. Dyck, Saskatoon, Saskatchewan, Canada

what is it
slipping into darkness
with the setting sun
that even my sixth sense
cannot detect

Victor Ortiz, Bellingham, WA

Hispaniola Isle:
a ship made of green valleys
and high rough sierras
where two nations* share rivers
and ancient hate in their souls

Ricardo J. Bogaert-Alvarez, Denver, CO

far beyond
our efforts to free that ship
in the Suez Canal
. . . waiting for a rising tide
and the supermoon

Robert Kusch, Piscataway, NJ

*Haiti and Dominican Republic

solitude . . .
where time rests
and floats—
a leaf
upon a lavender sea

Wendy Bourke, Burnaby, BC, Canada

darkening waves
surprise the sand with their embrace
disturb the night
then quietly retreat
while I dream of anemones

Gail Brooks, Laguna Beach, CA

geese squawk overhead
in perfect V formation
until the lead veers off
to take its place at the back
we humans need flying lessons

Pamela Shea, Sunland, CA

searching a clean place
in a corner of the field
away from the herd
a heifer prepares to birth
finding nature's way always

Mike Gallagher, Listowel, Ireland

in each
drop of dew
the sun
looks at itself
as in a mirror

Vasile Moldovan, Bucharest, Romania

the white fire
of the Kabbalah* nibbling
at my edges . . .
and in the darkness the form
of words as yet unspoken

Rebecca Drouilhet, Picayune, MS

tracings of light
find their way
through leaves
to spill on us
honey and stars

Susan Aurinko, Chicago, IL

I rise
on wings of flame
my pathway
to tranquility
littered with ash

Dru Philippou, Taos, NM

*an ancient Jewish mystical tradition

Tanka Sequences

the ogre

Joy McCall, Spinal Unit, Sheffield, England

a dark shape creeps
into my quiet room
and crouches low
I hear his shallow breath
slowly come and go

towards dawn
he drags his feet and hunches
beside my bed
in the lifting gloom
I see his monstrous head

from his piteous eyes
down his ruined face
tears fall
I wipe them and he shuffles off
muttering, down the hall

Escape

Mariko Kitakubo, Tokyo, Japan

riverside
unstoppable
spring wind
that day I escaped
from suicide

memory
of the violence
can survive
under water . . .
uncountable tough bubbles

don't try
to find me
I will be
nowhere . . .
somewhere in your memory

buds
are ready for
our future
sakura avenue
on our planet

An Afternoon in New Orleans

Michael Ketchek, Rochester, NY

drinking at the Monteleone
watching the blue bloods
and the blue jeaned
going round and round
at the Carousel Bar

the guy with the backwards
baseball cap and a Corona
among Martinis and Manhattans
Louie Armstrong says
it's a wonderful world

the tiger leaping
on the back
of the bar stool
a little higher
with every round

Lingering

Shelly Reed Thieman, West Des Moines, IA

you turn the heads
of coral bells
in summer
I await the ambrosia
of your lips

with stars as chaperones
we bathe in moonlight
your car in the drive at dawn
neighbors and trumpet vines
burn with gossip

the late autumn yard
low maintenance now
stripped bare
you'll always be
a bachelor button

this winter sky
turns its back on blue
many shades of gray now
you send a peace lily
an apology

(un)worthiness

Debbie Strange, Winnipeg, MB, Canada

a blue sand dune
discovered on Mars
the universe
gives me so much more
than I deserve

lost again
in the forest of mind
I tread warily
through macrocosms
of contrition

astronomers
describe a star's death
as spectacular
who is to say that
mine will not be so

With a Start

Michael Dylan Welch, Sammamish, WA

on the porch
out of earshot
we talk of dad's dying
how I will give the eulogy—
till he rises and shuffles near

frost overnight—
this morning's headlines
don't say
that my dad
has died

I wake up
with a start
this winter morning
wondering if my dad
was buried wearing shoes

Brave New World

Michelle Brock, Queanbeyan, NSW, Australia

Dempsy's ink sketch
circa 1824
a town crier . . .
twelve o'clock and all is well
on a cold Winchester night

sepia faces
stare into the present . . .
will our grandchildren
scroll through the cloud
to find us?

where to slot
this memory stick
left brain or right . . .
downloading family photographs
we are the elders now

precious moments
safely saved in jpeg files
if only
we could remember
the password to the olden days

Responsive Tanka

Still Hanging On

Amelia Fielden, Canberra , ACT, Australia
Marilyn Humbert, Sydney, NSW, Australia

bridging
hopes and reality
I facetime
distant grandchildren,
their phone passed back and forth

sepia photos
pasted three to a page
in the album
dad wearing short pants—
dust drifts through the attic

overcast days
leaves still hanging on
as autumn starts
we await our turns
for the magic vaccine

raucous noise
clouds of cockatoos
lift my mood …
the light and shade
of an uncertain future

over the park
a pandemonium
of parrots . . .
unperturbed, my old deaf dog
dawdles on the way home

mass rally
chanting protesters
wave placards
I am woman,
hear me roar …

Nights of Love

Genie Nakano, Gardena, CA
Kath Abela Wilson, Pasadena, CA

Akiko
wrote fifty tanka a day
I wonder
if she smoked
drank red wine

I found the wine
spilled in her tanka
a thousand lines
tangle her dark hair
after a night of love

no comb nor brush
can pass through my hair
gentle fingers
find their way in darkness
waves of undulating delight

my taste for love
unpins the upsweep
loosening
my dragonfly kanzashi
under the waterfall

the tear drops
from my burning eyes and lips
we are here
for each other
let the water fall

we drink
to this life of ours
clink of ice
in the hot springs
we have survived

Tanka Prose

Introduction

My response to Susan Weaver's email asking me if I'd like to be the next tanka prose editor was, "Wow … I'd love to … thank you." And here I am with the privilege of receiving your work and deciding which ones to publish.

As the submissions begin to trickle in, I gather my thoughts about what makes a good tanka prose.

When considering the mechanics of the genre, the analogy of teamwork comes to mind. The prose, tanka, and title work together, contributing their individual strengths and perspectives, in the spirit of cooperation. The writer manages the collective process of creation, easing any conflict, letting each voice have its say, until a satisfying outcome is achieved.

This leads me to a series of questions that may help bring some objectivity to the task of evaluating both my own and other people's work.

- Does the tanka enhance the prose?

- Does the prose enhance the tanka?

- Does the title give an extra layer of meaning?

- Are the title, prose, and tanka each working at their best?

- Are the title, prose, and tanka working well together?

But appreciation of any form of art is so subjective. I'm reminded of a renowned ballet company I saw at the Sydney Opera House years ago. Their performance could not be faulted; their technique was flawless. But, as the rest of the audience stood up and clapped their admiration for what these bodies had achieved, I could feel only the chill of something missing.

Was it soul? Was the spirit of the dance—its authentic, passionate, and vulnerable expression of what it is to be human, stifled by the focus on perfection?

With this in mind, I add to my checklist:

- Does the piece express something of the poet's experience?
- Is it satisfying to read?
- Does it feel authentic?
- Can I relate to this aspect of the human condition?
- Am I heartened, saddened, uplifted, amused, interested?
- Does the piece give me food for thought?
- Does it add to my appreciation and understanding of what it means to be alive today on this planet of ours?

Thank you to everyone who has contributed to this section of *Ribbons*. I have learned so much from reading your work, and I have, indeed, been given much food for thought.

—*Liz Lanigan*

The Road to Riches

Barbara Curnow, Canberra, Australia

Jim has finished his Saturday chores and rides his beaten-up bike along the road beyond the town. He takes his chores seriously because now he's man of the house. Father is in France, fighting. A canvas satchel hangs on Jim's back, and inside is a jam sandwich that he made himself. His mother made the jam from plums on the tree that shades the verandah.

> a pantry
> packed with pickles and preserves
> throughout the war
> her fruit and feelings
> all bottled up

Jim's riding to nowhere special, just likes riding. Heat rises and wobbles like jelly from the bitumen in the distance. He loves to bathe in the space of the open road, and he rarely sees a car or truck. He thinks his own thoughts, away from the persistence of his little sister, the clatter of the classroom, and the endless sound of the wireless that keeps his mum company, even in the early hours.

> war reports
> arrive on radio waves
> late at night
> she tries to tune in
> to her husband's heart

At the top of a hill, Jim stops to eat his sandwich. As he looks out across the paddocks, a glint of light catches his eye just a few feet away. With surprise, he realizes that a whole patch of roadside is sparkling in the sunshine. Bending down to touch the light, Jim sees that he's in the presence of diamonds!

A new bike flashes in his mind as he fills his bag. "Maybe there's enough for a car, too!"

When Jim gets home, he races to the kitchen and thrusts the bag into his mother's floury hands. "Diamonds!" he shouts. "I found them on the road!" But his mother sees only tiny cubes of shattered windscreen glass.

> she wants
> to let her son down
> gently . . .
> in her mind's eye
> her husband, his parachute

*　*　*

My Grandma kept Dad's "diamonds" for years. Eventually, she glued them together in a cylindrical shape. Grandad made a wooden base and rigged up the electrics, and so together they made a sparkling table lamp. It always captivated me as a child, and Dad never tired of telling me about the day he found diamonds!

Mandatory Mediation
David Rice, Berkeley, CA

Agreed Upon Facts: A day-long deluge, unprecedented at that time of year, roiled the river into a Class V rapid. The boats, *Short-term Greed* and *Fiddlin' While We Sink*, capsized. You, Officer Grimrod, waited until the next day to order helicopter reconnaissance.

Disputed Facts: Their relatives said you, Officer Grimrod, should have, and could have, prioritized the search and rescue. You said the economy was underwater, you were in meetings all afternoon, and that people going into the wilderness assume full responsibility for all risks involved.

> my grandson　　catches and releases　　a trout too small to keep
> 　　how can we stop losing　　what we'll never find?

A Day of Reckoning

Michael H. Lester, Los Angeles, CA

As a new birder, I've patiently waited for the past two months for a bird to visit my bird feeder. I move the cute miniature white bench with two trays for bird seed to the branch of a tree, aiming to provide more cover for the birds that I hope will visit for the black oil sunflower seeds. It leans against the tall picket fence, probably way too convenient for the neighborhood squirrels, as I discover when I catch one gorging herself on the seeds. I grab the ladder from the garage and move the feeder to a low branch further from the fence.

> precariously
> leaning over the third rung
> of the ladder
> I take pains not to fall
> the 20 inches into the mud

After a couple hours, the squirrel returns, engaging in all sorts of acrobatics to reach the seeds, but apparently giving up after several failed attempts. Soon after, I catch sight of my first bird visitor to the feeder, but she is too quick to fly away, and I cannot identify her.

With great expectations, I go to the kitchen window several times a day, looking for my fickle feathered friends.

> a lively pair
> of white-crowned sparrows
> peck at the seeds
> while a California towhee
> hops along the patio

As I prepare to photograph a frequently visiting black phoebe, we discover a darling female Allen's hummingbird with a broken wing, hopping in the hedges. We do everything we can to keep her alive while we try to find an emergency hospital for her, but she passes within a couple of hours. Wondering what I could have done better, I bury her in the backyard.

> the iridescence
> of her emerald feathers
> loses its luster
> as an eyedropper of nectar
> drips helplessly down her beak

The Untold Story
Chen-ou Liu, Ajax, ON, Canada

> the night
> shimmers on fresh snow . . .
> a frown
> wrinkles my forehead
> in the bedroom window

The German shepherd claims, "The old map of Taiwan on the wall shows where his heart lies."

"But not his mind," comes a rebuttal from the dog-eared Chinese-English dictionary on the coffee-stained desk. "He reads and writes in English every day."

With scarcely a moment's pause for reflection, the jar of salted bamboo shoots joins the discussion. "I think everything in his life is going okay . . . except for the food. He can't stand Canadian food."

> the stillness
> of another morning
> new layer
> upon layer of snow
> buries my immigrant past

Lifespan
Neena Singh, Chandigarh, India

in my solitude
a cool evening breeze
cradles me
with the tree boughs
swaying lullabies

When we moved to our new home, a potted pine arrived as a gift from
an old friend. We replanted it in our garden. Now, after two decades, it
is an ornamental landmark for visiting friends and home to a family of
playful squirrels, forever chittering as they scamper up and down.

feathery fronds
hold the full moon
in the gloaming
someone calls me
by a forgotten name

Clearing
Ann Corbett Burke, Orefield, PA

The stubbled edge of a cornfield parallels the banks of Jordan Creek.
Fog fills land and stream this late spring morning as warmth from
newly-turned earth mingles with creek water, still icy from its origin
near Blue Mountain. As the haze slowly lifts, birds take up their
morning's work.

after winter's dark,
absorbing the sun
my arms out-stretched—
a scarecrow
in spring fields

Shortcuts

Roger Jones, New Braunfels, TX

Whenever possible, I've tried to take a quiet way in life, to be low-key. Perhaps it was this inclination that led me to my first job as a delivery boy.

> taking shortcuts
> away from traffic noise
> I discover
> out of the way places . . .
> my boss will never know

In time, I developed particular favorites. Less travelled back roads, dormant buildings. At the graffitied railroad overpass, the road turned to skirt Willow Lake, whose cool surface revealed sunlit water and bright green lily pads. Just the briefest passing there, beneath a stand of oak trees, but sufficient to make me feel tranquil, present, good to go.

> river shallows
> along the bank
> on sudden whim
> all the silver minnows
> change direction

Emily's Dress*

Margaret Chula, Portland, OR

White cotton. Floor length, long sleeved, with pleats, lace trimmings, and a flounce at the bottom. Why did she wear white? Some say it was practical—easy to bleach—others say it was her sense of purity.

> mother-of-pearl buttons
> did she imagine a lover
> slowly, slowly
> unfastening them
> with sure, supple fingers

The stitching is perfect, even rows of matching threads.

> stab-bound
> and joined together
> with white string
> pages of her poems
> stitched into fascicles

A headless mannequin now models her dress. It stands in the corner of her second-floor room, looking out the open window.

> plein air painting
> of her orchard
> who can describe
> that *certain slant of light*
> on apple blossoms

Laid out in one of her white dresses, Emily was buried in a white casket.

all her life
she flirted with death
and darkness
when called back, a snowdrop
was placed upon on her breast

*On display at the Emily Dickinson Museum, Amherst, Mass.

Lost Voices
Kathryn Stevens, Cary, NC

August 14, 1941

The girl in the polka dot blouse and pleated skirt, that's my cousin at twenty. She's in a town somewhere near Prague. How comfortable she looks perching on the edge of a stone wall, smiling down at the camera. Yet she hugs herself tightly. Fingers of one hand dig into bare flesh. The other is closed. White-knuckle tight.

October 23, 1941

Here she is again. Standing in an intricately carved doorway. At her side is her new husband. Solemn, in a voluminous coat and black fedora pulled low on his brow. She looks older. Perhaps it's the shadows. Or her ill-fitting coat and beret. She avoids the camera's eye. In her hands, a bruised bouquet of white roses.

> looming
> over a tumble of houses,
> shadow of a cross . . .
> songs of lost children
> chalk dust in the wind

Reconnecting: Paroo-Darling National Park

Marilyn Humbert, Berowra Heights, NSW, Australia

Age-old coolabahs line the Darling River, giving shade in the hottest part of the day. We amble between their twisted arms that spread outwards and downwards; thready leaves brush my hair as I pass.

> flashes of pink
> tiny flowers
> peek
> from the understory
> watching our progress

The steep sided riverbank is barren grey clay, eroded through the cycles of drought and flood. The water level is receding, revealing snags and shoals of black granite.

> bubbles rise
> beneath river debris
> European carp
> stir the riverbed
> foraging muddy water

As shadows lengthen, we return to camp and watch flocks of cockatoos pleat, braid, and fold, criss-crossing the sky. Their raucous calls resound over the floodplains as night approaches.

> before sunset
> Major Mitchell's cockatoos
> return to roost
> glorious . . . the blush
> beneath white wings*

reconnecting
with our past, with each other
this peace
far from city lights
beneath southern stars

Note: Paroo-Darling National Park is about 50kms from Wilcannia, northeast NSW.

*A version of the fourth tanka appeared in *red lights*, January 2021.

Two Views

Mary Frederick Ahearn, South Coventry, PA

From your chair, across from mine, you see the watercolor of Grandfather's house, now long gone out of the family. For me, it's two iris and heron woodblock prints brought years ago from Tokyo.

Neither of us bothers to crane our necks to see the other's view; we already know it by heart.

But when you turn slightly to the right and I turn left, we see the same greening trees and holy blue sky out the windows. Another spring, and it's good and it's true.

so trivial
those blazing arguments
burnt to the silence
of cold mornings . . . now we share
the view from high windows*

* "High Windows" is a poem by Philip Larkin.

Through the Veil

Alexander Jankiewicz, Dixon, IL

I feel embarrassed to see their happy faces greeting me. I'm sure my rich relatives can spot a thrift store suit from a mile away. We haven't seen each other in years. Them rich. Me poor. *C'est la vie*, I guess.

I try to shrink my arms as I say hello and flash a smile. We trade pleasantries. We're all very pleased everyone is doing so well. We comment on how the bride and groom couldn't look happier.

"Rumor has it that he hasn't hit her in weeks."

empty pockets . . .
a scattering of rice
on the street
no one sees the pain
she hides behind a smile

Safe Pair of Hands

Sandra Renew, Canberra, Australia

Let's take you, River, out of the emotion. Let's view the you of you as a catastrophe badly managed. There is no good news, no happy end for you, while humans are so greedy.

Drought has given you a flogging, no doubt about that. And also, unseasonal seasons. There are fish with nowhere to go, our natives—Yellow Belly, Murray Cod, Bony Herring.

All your creeks, tributaries, gullies—like the fingers of a glove—short of flow. Its palm, Menindee Lakes, the Coorong, dying.

river trees
on thirsty banks
nails in your coffin
even with kid gloves
no safe pair of hands

Chaotic Fatigue

Robert Erlandson, Birmingham, MI

"If only one man dies of hunger, that is a tragedy. If millions die, that's only statistics." — Attributed to Josef Stalin

For millions, the impact of COVID-19 is real and profoundly painful. Yet for me, and millions more, the impact is felt only through ongoing media coverage, stories from family and friends, and the imposed safety restrictions. Responses to the pandemic have been framed as political and consequently have been fragmented and, at times, contentious. Still, arising from this divided sense of urgency come countless examples of people helping one another.

> unexpected moments
> explode
> disoriented
> our moral compass points
> to compassion and kindness

Stumpy

Bob Loomis, Concord, CA

I keep thinking
I see our sweet black cat
in familiar places . . .
the way grief plays
such cruel tricks

We've been fortunate not to lose human friends or family during the pandemic, but in just over a year, our cats, dear members of the family, have passed on. Three lived to around twenty years of age, so their deaths weren't unexpected. But the passing of twelve-year-old Stumpy came as a jarring surprise. She seemed to have discomfort when eating, so at first we thought she had a dental problem. When we took her to the veterinarian, we learned she had an aggressive mouth cancer that is common among cats and always fatal. There was nothing we could do as we watched her decline except give her comfort and pain relief. Two months after the diagnosis, when she could no longer eat, even by eyedropper, we had to help her die.

we bury her
beneath the flowerbed
she patrolled
hunting toads and lizards . . .
now all rest in peace

Changing Times

Joyce Futa, Altadena, CA

Today, waiting for curbside pickup of a dinner I ordered just to get out of the house, I noticed a young woman with a ponytail, wearing a black jacket on a very hot day. She was pushing a shopping cart across the parking lot. At first I thought she was going to her car to unload groceries. But then I noticed the stuffed bags and the large pieces of old cardboard.

She stopped beside a storage pod, sat on a ledge, and ate an apple, before getting up and pacing a small square, as if it were a room. "Like me in my living room," I thought, "she's trying to be normal."

A restaurant employee came out to retrieve something from the storage box. He chatted with her for a few minutes before asking her to leave. "No problem," she said, as she wheeled her cart away, her poise still intact.

> she remembers
> her cat, watching tv,
> her small apartment,
> as she gazes
> into the vast night sky

Thresholds

Dru Philippou, Taos, NM

the sun
swallows shadows
across the plateau
I strain to hear
whispers of the ancients

I enter the Puye Cliff Dwellings past clumps of mariposa lilies and owl's clover. Hand and footholds puncture the sheer tuff, patterns once familiar to the pueblos long, long ago. A calendar carved into the wall still tracks the seasons. On the mesa top, I stumble across evidence of communal living — garden plots, a reservoir, an irrigation canal, a sprawling village collapsed into emptiness.

Around 1580, drought forced the Puye to desert their homes and move into the valley near the Rio Grande, where they continue to live today as the Santa Clara Pueblo.

Leaning back against the rough bark of a piñon, I gaze toward Los Alamos, 23 miles away. There, the first atomic bomb was built. It was detonated 210 miles farther south, on a barren strip of land known as *Jornada del Muerto*. The Puye never imagined a sun hotter than the one they knew, hot enough to liquefy sand into glass, or a flash more brilliant than daylight. Their vision embraced corn plants transmuting sunlight into kernels.

a dark slow eddy
rises out of the past
I plunge
into a net of stars
in search of lost cousins

What's Going On?

Neal Whitman, Pacific Grove, CA

With much time of late spent at home with nowhere to go but medical appointments and walks along our Monterey Bay here in California, I found myself taking a look at boxes stored in closets and folders in file cabinets. Here and there I found handouts, reprints of journal articles, and other materials used to train me to be a docent at poet Robinson Jeffers' Tor House in Carmel, then to be a volunteer at the Monterey Hospice, and subsequently a guide at the Point Pinos Lighthouse, located in Pacific Grove, where I happen to live. I asked myself, "Why on Earth am I saving all this?" Out it all went into the recycle bin, and it was all gone by next Tuesday's barrel pick-up day.

This flashed a memory. On the afternoon of 9/11, I was sitting in my faculty office at the University of Utah, not able to settle down and do any work. As my eyes looked at two walls of bookcases, I began to grab books that I had not opened for years. Some were acquired as a graduate student in Ann Arbor, others for subsequent jobs in Jersey City and Chicago. Going back and forth, I tossed what was now obsolete into the outdoor dumpster. A colleague asked me what I was doing.

> all that is certain
> is that the future
> is uncertain—
> sometimes we have to
> make space for what is new

negative spaces
that once reflected light
this gallery
of ghosts haunting
smoke-stained walls

words/image(C)DStrange

Tanka and art by D. Strange

Poet and Tanka

Dreaming Room
Rebecca Drouilhet

The couple were galloping over the fields on strong horses, having gone to see the bush clover bloom. I could feel the wind in my hair as I rode with them. Everything about the poem seemed fresh and contemporary. When I finished the tanka, my eyes fell to the date it had been published: 691 C.E. It was part of the *Manyoshu*, an ancient Japanese record of early tanka, then called *waka*. I experienced them for the first time in 2012. Now, as Jenny Ward Angyal has written:

> deep in autumn
> I am haunted by horses
> the color of moonlight
> running like quicksilver
> in the wake of dreams

Presence 69, March 2021

She and others have inspired me to delve deep into the intuitive poetry derived from Japanese culture that has that indefinable something often referred to as the tanka spirit. For me, part of the tanka spirit is the intuitive space in the poem, the dreaming room that allows the reader to step into the poem with his/her own experiences and use imagination to "finish" the poem. Tanka are a cooperative effort between the author and the reader. In my opinion, this is part of what allows such a short poem to resonate with layers of depth and meaning.

I also came to know tanka as a form that could use language to get beneath language, as Michael McClintock did so brilliantly in this tanka:

I've this memory—
riding my father's shoulders
into the ocean,
the poetry of things
before I could speak

The Tanka of Michael McClintock
on Pinterest [2011-present]

Even a child who cannot yet speak, may, like readers of this tanka, intuitively grasp the poetry of a moment that defines meaning, significance, or beauty in a novel and profound way. William Least Heat Moon spoke eloquently of those defining times in his book, *Blue Highways*. For him, the moment was sharing a piece of old-fashioned buttermilk pie with new-found friends who had taken him in for the night on his long journey across the United States. For Michael McClintock, a childhood memory was poetry, and it became poetry for us as well, not through use of excessive or impressive words, but through sharing an image that takes us into the experience with him. Tanka is traditionally imagistic, possessing the power and magic of images that take us beneath words to the essence of experience.

Sometimes tanka can speak of the unspeakable by showing us the words that aren't there, as in this tanka by another person who has inspired me, the world-class Canadian poet Susan Constable:

orphan
widow widower
why not
a word for those
who lose a child?

Atlas Poetica #6, 2010

Noting the absence of a word eloquently reveals pain that is present but unaddressed in the English language and our shared cultures.

I came to tanka with the sensibility and culture of a woman of the Deep South in America. I have heard the South described as like the layers of an onion, where you can peel away a layer, only to find another layer and another. It is difficult to get to the bottom of the story here. Part of this is because communication is often subtle, with understanding implied rather than spelled out. Tanka often functions this way, too. Consider this tanka by Canadian poet, Chen-ou Liu:

> the pieces
> of his jigsaw puzzle
> litter the floor . . .
> winter moonlight slipping
> through the hospice window

> 2015 San Francisco International Competition
> Haiku, Senryu and Tanka – First Place, Tanka

What is left unsaid is powerful and may be the most important part of the poem. Most of us have unfinished business in life, almost as though our lives were an incomplete jigsaw puzzle. But in this poem, we see that the setting is a hospice. The author doesn't tell us that the patients have little time to accomplish their unfinished business. But what remains unsaid is revealed by the imagery of the puzzle and the knowledge we all possess about hospice and the endings in life. Our hearts allow us to identify with the unknown hospice patients, even as our empathy and intuition enable us to imagine how easily the poet's reality could be our own, or that of someone we love. Our imaginations arc over the small bridge of words in the poem, cross the space unspoken, and emerge as actualized realization and poetic and emotional truth. This quality, in my opinion, contributes to the dreaming room that characterizes the best in tanka poetry.

Chen-ou, who has won many international contests and awards, helped me write my first tanka. It was a failed haiku about a blues singer standing on the corner in New Orleans. He suggested I add two lines to a haiku that didn't really want to be a haiku, and *voila!* My life as a tanka poet was born. Chen-ou continued to encourage me. Because of his comments comparing the following poem to Georgia O'Keeffe's painting *Ladder to the Moon*, I was emboldened to enter it in the Tanka Time division of The Poetry Society of Tennessee's 62nd Annual Poetry Contest, where it won first place:

> if only
> I could reach the stars . . .
> the child in me
> climbs the first rung of a ladder
> that used to scrape the sky

Another early influence in my tanka life was the famous haiku and tanka poet, Jane Reichhold. I studied with her on her AHA Poetry site, eventually becoming a moderator of the AHA Poetry Forum. Jane was a wise and wonderful friend, and I was devastated when she died. After her death, I came across this tanka she wrote in 1990:

> a dead brown seed
> becoming in a muddy pot
> a white flower
> it is a lie you know
> about death, I mean

A Gift of Tanka, copyright 1990

This July will be the fifth anniversary of Jane's death. Often her poetry and other writing championed women in their struggles. Inspired by her and her AHA Poetry Forum tanka moderator, Jenny Ward Angyal, I wrote this poem and entered it in the Eighth International Tanka Festival in Tokyo, winning a certificate of merit:

> I seem to be
> a woman of glass . . .
> so many panes
> through which to see
> the bending of the light

And, in 2020, I entered TSA's Sanford Goldstein Annual Tanka Contest, in which the following poem won honorable mention, one of only three awards given in the contest that year:

> watercolor poppies
> blowing across the fields . . .
> why
> is it so hard
> to learn from history

So many times when we write tanka, we call back memories from our childhood and our common history, as I did in this poem. Our culture and our ancestry often figure in, as well. For me, these have been fertile grounds for exploration not only in my creative writing, but also in my life. Sometimes the lines between life and poetry blur and the magic happens. I once again curl my small toes through the morning glories twining up the columns of my grandparents' raised cottage. As a schoolchild, I buy red paper poppies from old soldiers and am transported to 1918, an era of pandemic and war. For a moment, I see watercolor poppies blowing across the field. And I am there, but cannot stay. We are always changing and so is life. Even when we're inspired by the past, nothing reminds us more than spring that change is eternal and we are ephemeral. I leave you with this poem of mine, inspired by a tanka written by Tekkan Yosano:

> the drift
> of white feathers plucked
> from a swan . . .
> spring wind scatters us, too,
> no trace left of who we are

NeverEnding Story, May 30, 2016

"This Very Air/Tanka"

Don Miller

"A snapshot of me in this moment" was the very minimal and seemingly simplistic definition of tanka Professor Sanford Goldstein gave to us in his creative writing class in 1982. Capturing one of these "moments"within the confines of a five-line lyric poem, then giving it room to expand with a shift and turn so that the reader is moved to journey beyond the initial image or emotion is the art of writing tanka. But to imply that this poetic form is simplistic would be glossing over what has eluded English-language tanka writers and scholars for a few decades now, and that is, "What makes an English-language tanka a tanka?"

M. Kei, in his paper, "A History of Tanka in English, Part I: The North American Foundation, 1899—1985," observes how difficult it is to understand tanka's historical development in English.

Indeed, it may be easier to follow the genre's evolution in Japan from *uta* (up to the late 7th century), into *waka* (late 7th and early 8th centuries through to the reform period), and then into modern Japanese tanka (the tanka reform period of the late 19th and early 20th centuries), than it is to understand what makes an English-language tanka a tanka. After decades of discussion and continued experimentation, there is still disagreement on what is an English-language tanka written by a non-Japanese poet. So, rather than attempting another paper defining such a tanka, this essay follows the path Goldstein blazed while unknowingly transforming modern Japanese tanka into modern English-language tanka.

The Bridge

"I think of myself as Takubokian. It was Takuboku who brought tanka closest to colloquial language while still guarding its poetic element. . ." —Sanford Goldstein, *This Tanka World*, "Afterword"

The distinctions "father," "grandfather,"and "master" of English-language tanka are all honors bestowed upon Sanford Goldstein. While there were attempts by non-Japanese poets to write tanka in English or other languages prior to Goldstein, it is his tireless and total immersion into tanka—as an educator in both the United States and Japan, a translator of tanka from Japanese into English, a prolific writer of the poetic form, but most importantly, a student of tanka—that provides us a path to understanding an English-language tanka. In his lifetime, Goldstein has become the bridge that's transformed the genre from modern Japanese tanka into modern English-language tanka by following one of the well-known reform poets of the early 20th century, Takuboku Ishikawa.

"This Very Air/Tanka"

In the following tanka from his first chapbook, *This Tanka World*, Goldstein provides us with a roadmap, of sorts, of what is tanka.

> this very air
> tanka
> no rhythm of 31
> no word-juggle
> only the deep of now

> Sanford Goldstein (46)

In this one poem, Goldstein gives us so much direction for writing English-language tanka, and yet he leaves us with an openness that tanka is this very air . . . the sphere of the moment surrounding us.

As a student of Takuboku, and like Takuboku and the other reform poets in Japan, Goldstein does not confine himself to mimicking the past in formal language on a narrow list of specific topics. Rather, as in the following tanka from *Four Decades on My Tanka Road*, he expands the moment, that sphere around us, to include everyday events and uses a commonplace voice.

first night
in the dark
I stumble for a place
to send my urine
natural

Sanford Goldstein (121)

No Rhythm of 31

"It was Takuboku who said the tanka need not restrict itself to thirty-one syllables." —Sanford Goldstein, *This Tanka World*, "Afterword"

Tamura out into the sea
Mishima with a sword
and others I could name with pills—
tonight
I count these ways of dying

Sanford Goldstein, (*This Tanka World* 19)

Although Goldstein can write thirty-one-syllable tanka, again, following the poets of modern Japanese tanka reform and their poetics, he does not restrict his tanka to a prescribed number of syllables (sound units). He lets the moment flow spontaneously, without counting.

"A poem gets its immediacy and we write it down. Often that is the way it is—an image, an event, a memory spontaneously inspires a poem that does not require juggling," Goldstein says in *This Short Life: Minimalist Tanka*. "Of course, there are times when we want to change a word or line, but the immediacy is still there." (6)

all day
my fear
of rebuke
what it might do
to my sensitive kid

Sanford Goldstein
(*This Short Life: Minimalist Tanka* 16)

No Word-juggle

"What happens when we are writing traditional tanka or one with longer or shorter lines is that the concentration is broken, for we are trying for a 5 or 7 syllable line . . . or for short-long-short-long-long."
—Sanford Goldstein, *This Short Life: Minimalist Tanka* (5)

Goldstein was not a student of a specific line pattern, nor did he teach it in his creative writing class at Purdue University. While many of his tanka may follow the line pattern of s/l/s/l/l that many English-language tanka poets favor today, he is not shackled to it, as many of his other tanka demonstrate. Goldstein stresses the sound or tone of each word or group of words and lets the natural flow of language dictate line length and the line break. As Goldstein says, if the line "spills" onto the next, so be it; capture the emotion of the moment, do not break the "immediacy of the moment by counting," do not break concentration.

Only the Deep of *Now*

"It was Takuboku who taught me that tanka is a diary of the emotional changes in a man's life." —Sanford Goldstein, *This Tanka World*, "Afterword"

Goldstein's somewhat minimalist definition for tanka, "a snapshot of me in this moment," may have been influenced by one of the other Japanese reform poets, Masaoka Shiki. As Makoto Ueda wrote in the

Introduction of *Modern Japanese Tanka*, "Shiki . . . proposed utilizing the principle of *shasei*, or 'sketch from life.'" In Shiki's opinion, "a poem expressive of the poet's self tended to be commonplace and trite unless that self was highly individualized, whereas a poem that faithfully observed life was always fresh because people's lives were never the same."

> never thought
> Buddha
> could sew
> until my wife's
> evening fingers

> Sanford Goldstein (*This Tanka World* 2)

Goldstein took tanka to the very root of the moment with his Zen meditation, to see, to observe, to look, and to write. And yet, within that "snapshot of the moment," which can be any one of the infinite moments of self within the surrounding sphere, tanka is in motion, exploding into the next moment, and striking off on unforeseen tangents! As the Zen Master, poet, and peace activist Thich Nhat Hanh has said, "We have more possibilities available in each moment than we realize."

Conclusion

A bridge between modern Japanese tanka and modern English tanka may be what we have been searching for, and it has been there all the time in Goldstein's example, in his writings. The modern English-language tanka is a short poem (*uta*); typically, but not always, written in five lines in English; expressed with an auto-biographical viewpoint in a colloquial language on any topic and without the constraints of counting syllables or following a particular line pattern. This is not to say tanka no longer follows a syllable count (sound units) nor utilizes line pattern or formal language. Rather, the Japanese reformists opened tanka up to be so much more with its colloquial language, and the breaking of constraints such as specific subject matter and counting. When written in English, the tanka's rhythm should follow what the writer hears, naturally, in the flow of the language without "word juggle," without breaking concentration on the moment. By utilizing the characteristics born out of Japan's tanka reform period, Goldstein bridges the gap between modern tanka written by Japanese poets and modern English-language tanka written by non-Japanese poets. As M. Kei noted in his paper, *The Problem of Tanka: Definition and Differentiation*, "Except for an isolated group within the New Wave period (1986–2005), who promoted, and are still promoting the return of tanka to its traditional *waka* origins with its narrow choice of models" and classical language of the Heian and early Kamakura periods, the English-language tanka follows the characteristics summarized above.

Understanding essential elements for an English-language tanka will guide us well as we travel with Goldstein along *"this tanka road."* However, we should consider these elements as being more like guidelines than hard and fast rules because, as with most literary genres, tanka is subject to adaptation, as it is influenced by the moment that surrounds us.

Book Reviews

A Triumphant Collection, *Perigee Moon*
Joshua Gage

Perigee Moon, Margaret Chula. Seattle, Washington: Red Mountain Press, 2021. ISBN: 978-1-952204-07-4. 92 pages, 5.25 x 8 inches. For a signed copy and 10% discount, order directly from the author at www.margaretchula.com (PayPal) or email her at margaretjchula@gmail.com with your mailing address. Cost is $20, postage paid in the United States.

Michael Dylan Welch writes in his introduction to *Perigee Moon*: "For those who might be new to tanka, Margaret Chula's *Perigee Moon* might serve as a model for how this poetry is done. And for those who have known tanka for decades and know Chula's vaunted place in its North American unfolding, this book will provide many rewards." It would be difficult to add anything to that sentiment. *Perigee Moon* gathers some of Chula's best tanka in one poignant collection, an example of a master artist at the peak of her form.

The book begins with the section "All Those Words for Love," a series of poems on love, relationships, lust, heartbreak, and the like. For those familiar with Yosano Akiko, Chula's poems are reminiscent of that past master. Tapping into the same feelings, she provides a great introduction to the collection and to tanka in general. These tanka move from the observational and amusing

> folding his clothes
> at the laundromat
> the backpacker
> checks out the Goth girl
> and then her underwear

to the more intimate and emotional

> squawk of a mallard
> her mate flies across the pond
> to comfort her—
> until this moment
> I didn't miss you at all

It's a moving section, and while Chula doesn't stray away from intense emotions, she doesn't let her poetry become saccharine or maudlin.

The next grouping, "Spots of Rust," depicts Chula's relationship with her mother. These tanka are emotional in a different way as we see Chula wrestle with her mother's decline into illness and eventual death. The shift from the first section to this one is extreme. That seems to be what Chula is aiming for. Again, readers see her humor

> in her mid-nineties
> Mother shuffles her walker
> across the lawn
> *there must be something*
> *I need at this tag sale*

as well as her ability to capture those deep, resonant emotions in the minimal space of tanka

> Mother's death day
> look how hopefully
> chickadees flit
> to the empty feeder
> again, again, and again

This is another strong segment, sampling Chula's tanka that dive deep into the emotions of a child who's watching her parent age and die, wrestling with all the complications of those moments.

The third part, "Keepsakes," seems dedicated to memories. It's dark and angry, more biting than the previous two. Whereas those sections were filled with the big, strong emotions of love and loss, "Keepsakes" focuses on uglier memories, those things that even years later we cannot forget or let go. Even when the poems aren't directly about a specific event, Chula manages to slip in those acerbic feelings that readers will find all too familiar.

> tomato starts
> first the yellow blossoms
> then the red fruit—
> be careful, my sweet
> of who you let pluck you

This is an engaging and bold portion because Chula deals with emotions that readers will identify with, but that most people will argue are too ugly for poetry. Chula's tanka prove that not only are these feelings part of the human experience, but that handled well, they can be poetic.

"All the Day's Colors," the fourth grouping, depicts moments in nature. This is a softer section and more introspective than the previous three, but it feels like a well-needed break after all those strong emotions. There are light-hearted poems here and some that deal with the honest brutality of the natural world.

> waning moon
> milkweed seeds burst
> from their pods
> the luna moth taut
> in the owl's beak

Here Chula showcases her depth as a poet, and that she's not just a one-trick-pony tapping into big emotions only. She's equally capable of handling the more subtle but still poignant events in the natural world with her words, almost reminiscent of Mary Oliver's work.

end of summer
I lie in the hammock
in my white lace skirt
and watch the hibiscus
fold up its petals

These moments seem private but no less striking. They are often more observational, less focused on the speaker's emotions than on the flora and fauna being experienced. This creates a pleasing arc in the book and a welcome respite for the reader.

The final section, "Footloose and Fancy-Free," draws on Chula's extensive travels. These tanka wander across the globe, from Sri Lanka to Greece to Poland to Japan.

sacred Mt. Fuji
home of the Immortals
hidden in clouds—
like Issa's snail
I climb it slowly, slowly

Having run the gamut of emotions, readers are whirled around the world in a kaleidoscope of experiences. It makes a fitting end for a triumphant collection of tanka.

All About Love
Michael Dylan Welch

Love: The British Haiku Society 30th Anniversary Members' Tanka Anthology, edited by A. A. Marcoff. Barking, England: British Haiku Society, 2020. ISBN 978-1-906333-13-3. 36 pages. £4.00 plus shipping from http://britishhaikusociety.org.uk.

Introducing this collection, the editor reports, "When I was walking by the famous shrine at Kashima in 1980, I asked my friend Mr. Kudo which he preferred—haiku or tanka?—and he answered without hesitation, 'tanka, because they are more romantic.'" And this may well be why this pleasing anthology has a theme of love. The British Haiku Society has always included tanka as part of its haiku journal, *Blithe Spirit*, but as a gift to its members in celebration of the society's thirtieth anniversary, the society decided to publish first-time anthologies for tanka and haibun in addition to its usual haiku/ senryu members' anthology—and this is the tanka collection.

Editor A. A. Marcoff observes that tanka "are perhaps closer to western poetry than haiku are," and adds that "tanka may divide into two parts—'the poet sees,' and 'the poet reflects.'" The book features eighty-five poets, most from the United Kingdom, but with surprises from around the world. Poems are arranged alphabetically by each poet's first name.

As a sampling, here is every tenth poem, illustrating the varieties of love in our lives:

> what one was
> must still be there
> in our hearts
> the whisper of wind
> voiced by trees
>
> *Bob Lucky (Saudi Arabia)*

> the way the berths
> of his sailboat curve
> inward at the bow:
> all night your breath
> cool on my forehead
>
> *Dee Evetts (UK)*

two herons
circle the lake
wartime romance
he clears away grass
from her grave

Graham Duff (UK)

my son shows me
a caterpillar cloud
in autumn-blue sky . . .
the way things change
in unexpected ways

John Barlow (UK)

along my spine
the touch of his piano
floats me to a place where
silence becomes butterflies
when the world's hinge swings shut

Linda Jeannette Ward (USA)

alone,
his wife in a nursing home,
he lingers
over a cappuccino . . .
perusing *lonely hearts page*

Mary Gunn (Ireland)

by the old bridge
two lovers pause
relive
lost innocence
play Pooh Sticks

Peter Morriss (UK)

enough now
just to know
you are here . . .
my fingertips seek
your night-warm skin

Susan King (UK)

Although the poems submitted for this collection were intended to be about love (without mentioning the word), it seems true that tanka itself is often a love poem. Love was the most common theme in ancient Japanese tanka, and here we can see the theme's continuing vitality in the book's joyous, heartwarming, yet occasionally heart-wrenching poems. Here's one more from this recommended book, about a kind of love at the end of life:

growing old
in a corner of my garden
her favourite flowers
seeds scattered with the ashes
and the evening breeze

Susan Spooner (Canada)

News and Announcements

2021 TSA Membership Anthology

Members, please send your tanka! The Tanka Society of America is delighted that Michael H. Lester will edit the 2021 TSA members' anthology. The submission window for entry is June 1 to July 31, 2021, and Michael will respond to all submissions by August 31. All 2021 TSA members who submit five (unpublished) tanka will be guaranteed inclusion in the anthology. It will be published this fall and sent free to all current members. To submit, (members only) please see the guidelines on our website: http://www.tankasociety ofamerica.org/tsa-anthologies/2021-anthology-submission-guidelines.

Index of Contributors

Pat Geyer, 18
Mel Goldberg, 55
Sanford Goldstein, 117
LeRoy Gorman, 42, 64
JeanMarie Gossard, 70
Vince Gotera, 34
Joyce S. Greene, 24
Martin Grenfell, 65
Mary Gunn, 128
Lucia Haase, 57
Johnnie Johnson Hafernik, 34
Hazel Hall, 66
Jon Hare, 68
Charles Harmon, 22, 75
Carole Harrison, 37, 71
William Hart, 75
Michele L. Harvey, 29, 67
Marilyn Hazelton, 43
David He, 77
David Lee Hill, 21, 60
C. William Hinderliter, 56
Ruth Holzer, 19, 59
Louisa Howerow, 52
Elinor Pihl Huggett, 23, 55
Marilyn Humbert, 89, 103
Lakshmi Iyer, 52
Rick Jackofsky, 59
Roberta Beach Jacobson, 32, 78
Alexander Jankiewicz, 105
Peter Jastermsky, 43, 50
Roger Jones, 100
Mary Kendall, 24, 73
Michael Ketchek, 39, 84
Keitha Keyes, 26
Susan King, 129
Mariko Kitakubo, 39, 83
Kathy Kituai, 10

Mari Konno, 43, 49
Robert Kusch, 17, 79
Liz Lanigan, 23, 67, 93
Kat Lehmann, 50
Michael H. Lester, 4, 20, 97
Ryland Shengzhi Li, 76
Chen-ou Liu, 17, 61, 98, 114
Gregory Longenecker, 40, 68
Bob Loomis, 23, 107
Bob Lucky, 12, 35, 59, 127
Jeanne Lupton, 32, 64
Kathleen Caster Mace, 69
Elizabeth Martens, 44
Giselle Maya, 11, 41
Joy McCall, 17, 82
Michael McClintock, 14, 28, 47, 113
Robert B. McNeill, 39
Don Miller, 117
Vasile Moldovan, 81
Oscar Montes, 52
Mike Montreuil, 22
Lenard D. Moore, 40, 56
Peter Morriss, 129
Genie Nakano, 27, 91
David F. Noble, 28, 75
Sarah Ockrim, 65
Helen Ogden, 36, 65
Victor Ortiz, 34, 79
Trilla Pando, 41
Bill Pauly, 70
James B. Peters, 20, 53
Dru Philippou, 34, 81, 109
Madhuri Pillai, 33, 55
Maryalicia Post, 60
Patricia Prime, 57
Nu Quang, 27
John Quinnett, 38

Submission Guidelines

Submissions to *Ribbons*, the Tanka Society of America's journal, are open to TSA members and non-members alike.

Ribbons submission deadlines are in-hand no later than

April 30: Spring/Summer Issue
August 31: Fall Issue
December 31: Winter Issue

The *Ribbons* editors will respond to all submissions within one month of the submission deadline.

Your submissions must not be under consideration elsewhere, submitted to any contest, or previously published anywhere at any time, including online; however, tanka posted to online workshop lists or on Facebook are permissible. All rights revert to authors upon publication, except that the TSA reserves the right to reprint content from its publications on TSA social media sites and its website.

Ribbons seeks fresh material of the highest standard to present to our readers. Any tanka with a sensibility that distinguishes the form will be considered. Therefore, we welcome different syllable counts, varying individual styles and techniques, and are open to diverse yet appropriate subject material. We also welcome essays that offer fresh insights and information.

Tanka: You are welcome to submit *either* up to ten unpublished, original tanka *or* two tanka sequences (not more than six tanka per sequence) for each issue, as well as essays, interviews, news, and announcements. Email submissions are preferred, using the subject heading "*Ribbons* Submissions." Send to: RibbonsEditor@gmail.com. You may also submit by postal mail:

Susan Weaver, *Ribbons* Editor
127 N. 10th St., Allentown, PA 18102

Tanka Prose: Send one tanka prose piece to Liz Lanigan, our tanka prose editor, at tankaproseeditor@gmail.com. Please enter *"Ribbons Submission"* in the subject line. While submissions by email are preferred, you may also submit tanka prose by postal mail:

> Liz Lanigan, *Ribbons* Tanka Prose Editor
> 38 McClure Street, EVATT ACT 2617, Australia

Prose count should not exceed 300 words. Number of tanka is flexible (within reason and when in service to the whole). Please include a creative title.

Regarding frequency of submission, tanka prose writers whose work is accepted are asked to hold off from contributing tanka prose again for at least one submission period after publication. This policy gives more tanka prose poets a chance to share their work. It also lets us represent the many ways tanka prose is being written today.

Book Reviews: Please send books for review to our editor, Susan Weaver, by postal mail:

> Susan Weaver, *Ribbons* Editor
> 127 N. 10th Street, Allentown, PA 18102

If you wish to query about a book review, please email Susan Weaver at RibbonsEditor@gmail.com. Likewise, if you mailed a book for review in past months and/or queried about a review, and did not receive a response, please email to the same address so any oversights can be remedied.

Note: These guidelines do not apply to submissions to the Tanka Café column (which is open to TSA members only). For Tanka Café guidelines, see a current issue of *Ribbons* or the TSA website. Please send your Tanka Café submission to Michael McClintock at MchlMcClintock@aol.com with "Tanka Café" as the subject heading or by postal mail to: Michael McClintock, 1830 N. Bush Avenue, Clovis, CA 93619.